RUBANK EDUCATIONAL LIBRARY No. 80

Soloist Folio

FOR
Eb OR BBb BASS (TUBA - SOUSAPHONE)
with Piano Accompaniment

CONTENTS

RUBANK®

HAL•LEONARD®
CORPORATION
7777 W. BLUEMOUND RD. P.O.BOX 13819 MILWAUKEE, WI 53213

Out On the Deep

Piano

FREDERIC N. LOHR
Arr. by G.E. Holmes

Allegro moderato

The Jolly Peasant

FANTASY

Piano

R. SCHUMANN
Arr. by G.E. Holmes

The Jolly Peasant - 3

Bombastoso

CAPRICE

VANDER COOK

Piu mosso

TRIO

not too fast

The Marines' Hymn

Air Varie

Piano

L. Z. PHILLIPS
Arr. by G. E. Holmes

"MARINES HYMN" Copy-

Alla marcia (♩ = 112)

right U.S. Marine Corps. Used by permission

In the Hall of the Mountain King

from

PEER GYNT SUITE

EDVARD GRIEG
Arr. by G.E. Holmes

In the Hall of the Mountain King - 3

In the Hall of the Mountain King - 3

Forget Me Not

INTERMEZZO

Piano

ALLAN MACBETH
Arr. by G.E. Holmes

Forget Me Not - 4

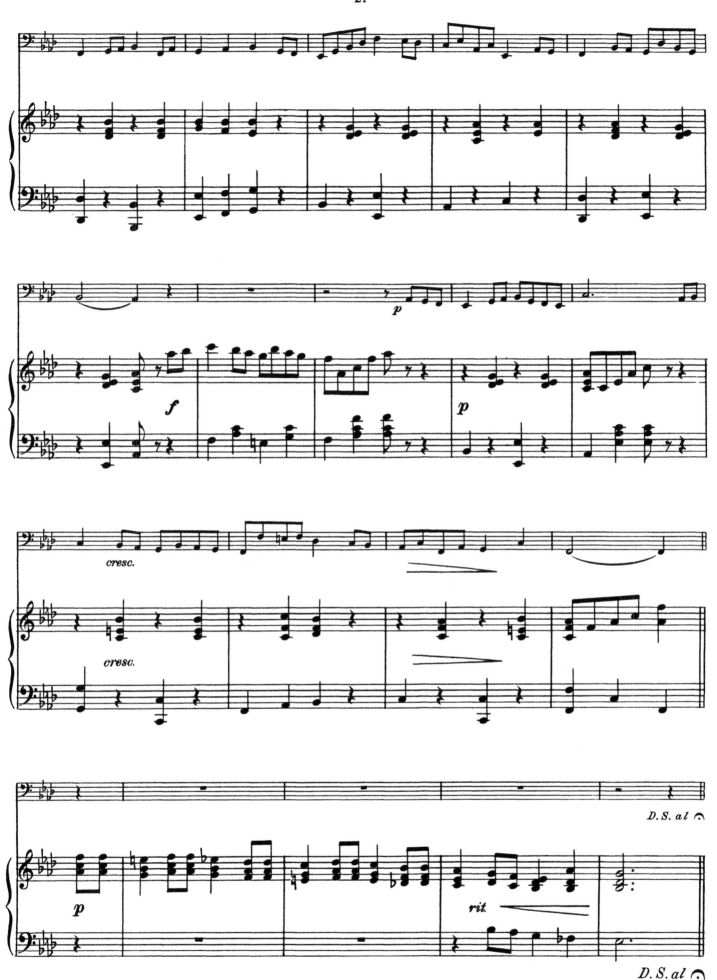

Forget Me Not - 4

Bedouin Love Song

Piano

CIRO PINSUTI
Arr. by G. E. Holmes

Allegretto moderato

Bedouin Love Song –3

Bedouin Love Song - 3

Toreador's Song

from

CARMEN

Piano

GEORGES BIZET
Arr. by G.E.Holmes

Allegro moderato (♩ = 108)

Toreador's Song - 4

Rocked in the Cradle of the Deep

Air and Variations

Solo for E♭ or BB♭ Bass (Tuba)

Piano

E. DE LAMATER

THEME

Copyright MCMXXXVII by Rubank, Inc., Chicago, Ill.
International Copyright Secured

Stupendo

Concert Polka

Piano

N. K. BRAHMSTEDT

Copyright MCMXXXVII by Rubank, Inc., Chicago, Ill.
International Copyright Secured